DATE DUE

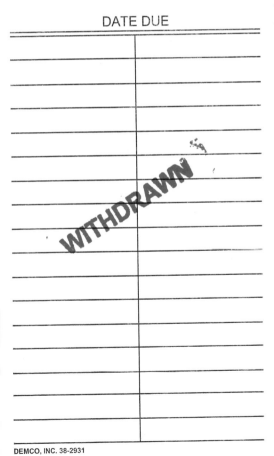

Praise for *Pretty Good Presentation*

"TJ Walker takes the fear factor out of speaking to the media and live audiences and clearly explains the secrets of great communicators like Reagan and Clinton. The best part is, what he teaches you really works when you put it to practice."

—**Hakan Lindskog**
TimeLife

"TJ's latest book is chock full of helpful hints that will help anyone who reads it!"

—**David Winters**
Wintergreen Funds

"TJ Walker is the leading media trainer in the world."

—**Stu Miller**
Producer, Viacom TV

"TJ Walker's single-minded devotion to presentation training has made him the #1 expert for executives seeking guidance on speaking to the public and media."

—**Bob Bowdon**
Anchor/Reporter, Bloomberg TV

"Over the years I've been a fan of TJ Walker and his rigorous approach to media training. TJ is clearly a veteran of the broadcast and print interview world and his tips are well worth reading. I know I've learned some new strategies."

—**Edward Aloysius Moed**
Peppercom, Inc.

"TJ Walker was able to help my entire team operate more efficiently [and] maximize their message penetration to their audience."

—**Michael Gallant**
EMC

HOW TO GIVE A PRETTY GOOD PRESENTATION

A Speaking
Survival Guide for
the Rest of Us

HOW TO GIVE A PRETTY GOOD PRESENTATION

A Speaking Survival Guide for the Rest of Us

TJ WALKER

WILEY

John Wiley & Sons, Inc.

For general information on our other products and services or for technical support, please contact our Customer Care Department within the United States at (800) 762-2974, outside the United States at (317) 572-3993 or fax (317) 572-4002.

Wiley also publishes its books in a variety of electronic formats. Some content that appears in print may not be available in electronic books. For more information about Wiley products, visit our web site at www.wiley.com.

ISBN 978-0-470-59714-9 (cloth)
ISBN 978-0-470-87537-2 (ebk)
ISBN 978-0-470-87538-0 (ebk)
ISBN 978-0-470-87539-9 (ebk)

Printed in the United States of America

10 9 8 7 6 5 4 3 2 1

To Leah Lagos, who accepted my pretty good marriage proposal presentation.

CONTENTS

ACKNOWLEDGMENTS

I would like to acknowledge my mother Patti for all she did to nurture, aid, and promote my life and career over her lifetime. She died unexpectedly in March 2010, and I will forever remember the fantastic "thank you" speech she delivered to family and friends at her 75th birthday party just months before her death. She was my number one fan and supporter for 47 years and will be sorely missed by me and everyone who knew her.

I'd also like to thank all of the day-in and day-out contributions from my team at Media Training Worldwide and TJ Walker Speaking: Kris Gentile, Mike Bako and Jennifer Wallerstein. They turn work into fun each day and together we help the world speak a little better.

My friends who are always there for me, thanks. Rich Gladstone, Joe McHugh, and Bob Bowdon, you have put up with me for decades and there is no reprieve in sight.

Thanks also to my fiancée and soon-to-be wife Dr. Leah Lagos for all of her time, love and joy you bring to my life.

INTRODUCTION

How to Give a Pretty Good Publication

Shortly after my book ***TJ Walker's Secret to Foolproof Presentations*** went to number one on the *USA Today* bestseller list, I received a call from an editor. "Hey TJ, congrats on the book; but what about all the people who don't want to give a "Foolproof Presentation?"

What on earth did that mean? I responded, "What?"

She responded, "Well, your book talks about how to give a foolproof presentation; and it seems like all the books on speaking want to show readers how to get a standing ovation, give an exceptional presentation, or an insanely great presentation. What about the 99 percent of the world who don't want to be the next Tony Robbins? What about the people who either don't like giving presentations or fear public speaking and just want to get through the darn thing? What about all the people who just want to give a pretty good presentation, but not one that will set the world on fire? Don't they have a right to get what they want?"

And that's how this book was born.

If you want to become the next Bill Clinton, Ronald Reagan, Barack Obama, or Winston Churchill, then this book is *not* for you (because there are already a gazillion books written for you). If there is nothing you would rather do than deliver a PowerPoint to 1,000 people, give a toast to a wedding party of 500, or do a live interview on CNN, then this book is *not* for you (although I understand where you're coming from, because you're just like me). This book is written for normal people—and I readily admit I'm not one. I was the nerdy, dweeby junior high school student council president who loved giving speeches in front of 1,200 students at age 13.

I'm not going to waste your time giving you lengthy and difficult exercises designed to make you the next king of the motivational speaking circuit, as seen on late night infomercials. Instead, I'm going to give you the fastest, shortest, simplest ways of giving a pretty good presentation. Period.

I work with thousands of businesspeople, political leaders, United Nations officials, and beauty queens from six continents every year; and they have varying skills and goals when it comes to their speaking abilities. Everything I'm going to share with you is based on real-world experience helping people just like you, most of whom were sent to my presentation workshops reluctantly, usually by a boss who believed in them and wanted to help them gain skills needed to advance to the next part of their careers.

While there are a million different kinds of speakers and speaking situations in the world, I boil everything down into three main categories. First, there are the truly awful speakers who do boring data dumps. No one in the audience remembers anything from the message or the speaker other than that the speaker was boring and perhaps seemed nervous. This is the widest variety of all presenters in the world.

Second, there is the category of truly outstanding speakers. Whether it is someone on the international level like a Steve Jobs in business or Tony Blair in politics, these people have the ability to make any presentation truly memorable, engaging, interesting, and useful, and convey confidence, warmth, and likeability in the process. At the local level, your own mayor or head of the chamber of commerce may be like this. This is a small group of people, typically less than 1 percent of all speakers.

There is also a third group of people. These individuals are able to speak much better than the first group, but not nearly as well as the second group. They come across as professional, competent, and understandable, and can get to their points in a concise manner and have their points remembered. No one was ever moved to tears after listening to someone in this third group give a presentation; no one ever fell asleep while they were presenting, either. Members of this third group don't spend days preparing and rehearsing their speech the way Ronald Reagan did or the way Steve Jobs does, because they have too many other demands on their time at work and home. Giving a spellbinding speech simply isn't a top priority in their life. However, they *are* willing to spend anywhere from five minutes to one hour preparing their speeches; they know they have to in order to get what they want done for their career and in life. They want to eliminate the pain of giving an awful presentation, and avoid having to spend dozens of hours rehearsing. Members of this third group simply want to give a pretty good presentation—and they do it, every time.

If you want to be a member of the third group— the category of speakers who can give a pretty good presentation—then this book is for you. I promise that if you follow the simple and straightforward lessons I have laid out for you, you will consistently be a pretty good presenter. You will never fail to get a promotion or win a new client just because your presentation skills are considered substandard. You will never have to spend another sleepless night before a big speech worrying that you will bomb, because you will know that it will no longer be possible for you to bomb.

I am going to respect your time, because I know that speech making is not your number one concern. Therefore, I'm only going to give you the most important and least time-consuming tips to make you a better presenter.

Here's what else you will learn:

- The most common blunders in every speaking situation that plague most presenters.
- The difficult and time-consuming advanced techniques that professional speakers use **that you won't have to use**.
- The simple, easy, fast way to give your presentation better than 80 percent of your colleagues so that you can sit down and get on with the rest of your busy life.

Shall we begin?

HOW TO GIVE A PRETTY GOOD

A Speaking
Survival Guide for
the Rest of Us

GOOD

PRESENTATION

Part One

First Thing First

1

YOUR
INTRODUCTION

*Should I Be Introduced Before Giving a
Presentation or Not Introduced at All?*

By all means, be introduced—especially if you are talking to more than a couple of people. However, keep the purpose of the introduction in mind: to give people a sense of why they should care about you and what you have to say. The intro should make the audience practically salivate in anticipation of hearing you speak.

Big tip: Don't let anyone else write or create your introduction; do it yourself.

So how do you write the ideal introduction for yourself? I think the best approach is to create a Venn diagram. In one large circle, write down every single fact about yourself—everything from your resume to your high school honors and so on. Next, write down everything in a circle that could possibly motivate someone in the audience who doesn't know you to want to listen to you speak on this topic. Finally, list everything in a circle that makes you uniquely qualified to speak on this subject.

Now, look at your Venn diagram and see how many bullet points overlap. Chances are, there's only about 30 seconds' worth of material that is genuinely important to both you and your audience, *and* makes the case for why you are uniquely qualified to talk about it. Thirty seconds is plenty—maybe a minute if you've won the Nobel Prize.

Don't have someone introduce you by listing every award, accomplishment, and degree you've ever earned. No one cares, except for your parents, and they already know because they had to foot the bill for everything.

Don't leave the intro up to chance. Type it out in very large font (18 point or bigger) and hand it to the person introducing you (keep the sentences really short or use bullet points).

If no one is there to introduce you, then do it yourself. Just don't act embarrassed, and don't go on too long. Again, stick to the most relevant 30 seconds' worth of facts following the above criteria; and then get to the meat of the speech.

Long introductions are hard for you to write, hard for the person introducing you to deliver, and hard for the audience to listen to. This really is one of the times where it pays to be concise; now you'll have more time to talk about what really interests your audience. Chances are that's your topic—not you.

2

THE TONE

HOW DO I SET THE TONE FOR A PRESENTATION?

Tone, schmone; there is no such thing as a formal or informal presentation! There is no such thing as a technical presentation or a PowerPoint presentation. There are only two kinds of presentations in the entire world: interesting or boring. So which one is yours going to be?

SHOULD IT BE FORMAL OR INFORMAL?

The easiest way to create a boring presentation is to try to be "formal." This typically means you have removed any and all humor, feeling, examples, stories, and interesting vignettes from your presentation. Why on earth would you want to do that?

You do want your presentation to be "informal" in the sense that you are as interesting and fun and as unpompous as you are when speaking to a friend at a comfortable restaurant. While the topic you're covering may be serious—say, financing of your company's new factory—the way you talk can be as informal and friendly as if you were talking about baseball or "Dancing with the Stars" with a friend over dinner.

Formal often means reading a speech. When is the last time you enjoyed listening to someone reading a presentation in front of you? Chances are you had to be carried out of the room on a stretcher because people thought you had died of boredom after about five minutes.

Do not forget to use contractions when you are giving a presentation—or rather, ***don't*** forget to use contractions when giving a presentation. Using contractions will make you seem informal and likeable. Not using contractions will make you seem like a silly, pompous TV sitcom butler who is the butt of jokes and ridicule. Trying to be formal is going to make you uncomfortable; and that's the last thing you need. I want to make your life easy, and it's a lot easier to talk in the same informal manner you do with friends and family on a daily basis.

Presenting in an informal manner does not mean being lazy or turning into a slob. It's not a license to put your feet on the table or wear the old warm-up suit your mother gave you for your birthday nine years ago. You should dress formally if the occasion merits it; but when it comes to speaking, be informal. That means using simple, short words, short sentences, and not being afraid to repeat yourself.

When in doubt about whether to be formal, just remember: you are unlikely to ever, ever hear the following 11 words: "I sure am glad that speaker gave us such a *formal* presentation."

3

TAILORING YOUR SPEECH

SHOULD I TAILOR THE SPEECH FOR THE TYPE OF AUDIENCE?

If you simply want to give a pretty good presentation, don't waste time trying to figure out how to tailor your speech to your audience in terms of stories versus facts. Audiences around the world are all the same: they want stories that involve relevant ideas and facts that affect them. If all you do is present the facts, ma'am, there is an excellent chance your speech will come up short—and be incredibly boring and instantly forgotten.

TELLING PERSONAL STORIES VERSUS JUST THE FACTS

It is true that different audiences will tell you they like different styles as far as facts versus concepts versus stories. Ignore them. You do, however, want to tailor your *messages* to your audience; so by all means, do some research and find out what messages your audience is interested in, what questions they need answers to, and what problems they have that you might be able to solve. Then give them a presentation that is focused on a handful of messages that are important to them and to you, a story for each, and the most essential relevant facts. I know you've heard that one size doesn't fit all, but in this case, it really does. Messages may differ from audience to audience, but the best way to tailor your speech to an audience really does not change.

Don't be fooled when people tell you their audience is different because everyone has advanced degrees or are "industry insiders." Yes, their audience is different because every audience is different; but audiences never differ in the way people think they do. It's just that certain messages will bore them or interest them in various ways. But audiences are more alike than they are different; and the number one way in which most audiences are alike is that they are easily bored to death by a presenter who tries to "just stick to the facts" and leaves out all of the examples, stories, and vignettes.

4

KICKING THINGS OFF

*How Do I Kick Off a Speech? A Joke?
A Personal Story? Help!*

The beginning of a presentation is a touchy time. On the one hand, you are feeling nervous and might not be quite sure of yourself yet. On the other hand, the audience is nervous for a different reason: they are worried that you might be about to bore them to death and perhaps they should have brought more reading material, called in sick, or located some cyanide tablets. Everyone—including you—is on edge!

So that's why people like to start off a presentation with a joke. The only problem is that it's hard to be funny. My advice? Don't bother. After all, you aren't trying to get booked at the local Comedy Cellar on Saturday night; so don't give yourself all the pressure of trying to be funny on demand. You aren't a trained seal!

To be a pretty good presenter, you only have to make one decision about the following two options when it comes to starting your speech: (1) Are you going to talk about yourself? Or (2) are you going to talk about something that is remotely interesting to your audience?

If you're George Clooney, you can talk about yourself and people will find that interesting. However, if you are not a famous movie star, my recommendation is to discuss something of interest to your audience within the first five seconds of opening your mouth.

Most awful presenters spend the first five minutes saying the following boring stuff: "I'm happy to be here; thank you for that wonderful introduction. Here's what I studied in college, here's the boring history of my company, here are all the cities my company is in that you don't care about because you are in this city, here are the 14 points I'm going to cover in my presentation today (and since I will cover them later you don't have to pay attention now), and the bathrooms are down the hall and on the right. Have you fallen asleep yet?

To be a pretty good presenter, all you have to do is focus your attention on your audience instead of yourself at the beginning of a presentation. Imagine if you started a presentation with, "I was just in the hallway talking to Jim and he said 'TJ, I've just lost my best customer because he says my prices are too high. What can I do?'" That might not be a brilliant opening to a speech, but it's pretty good, and here's why:

1. Jim is listening because I've mentioned him by name.
2. Everyone else can relate to a problem that one of their colleagues has; and so now *they* are listening.
3. Everyone is surprised that this is the first thing out of my mouth because they expected me to stare down at notes and go through the usual clichés of being happy to be there and so on.
4. I appear to be supremely confident because I seem to be speaking off-script and ad-libbing (even though the opening was planned).

Let's say you don't get to the room in time to ask anyone a question in advance. That's okay. When you start your presentation, begin by asking everyone a question and see what responses you generate. Again, you won't seem like you are starting with boring, canned clichés, so you'll seem pretty good in comparison to most speakers. Just make sure that the questions you ask your audience are real questions and not just cheap gimmicks to get people to raise their hands. I can't stand it if a speaker starts off a presentation by asking, "How many of you would like to make more money and work fewer hours each week?" Well, who wouldn't? Duh! Questions like this are insulting because they come across as manipulative and don't seem designed to generate thoughtful answers.

As long as you can think of one interesting question for your audience or have one interesting fact or message for them, you will always have a pretty good beginning to your presentation.

5

THE GAME PLAN

Should I Outline the Key Points of My Presentation to My Audience?

No—why make it harder on yourself if you forget a point? If you never tell your audience all the points you are going to cover in advance, then they will never know if you left one out. Plus, you will never feel pressure to remember your point number 12 from some complex outline. Sure, there are some world-class speakers like Apple's Steve Jobs who believe that you should always outline for your audience. However, if your audience isn't writing down everything you say word for word—and that rarely happens—then outlining your presentation doesn't help them or you.

My recommendation is for you to just focus on making one point at a time; this is easy for you and your audience. When you finish with one point—by giving examples, telling stories, and the like—then move to the next point. After you have finished covering the handful of most important points you wanted to cover, sit down. You will have given a pretty good presentation.

6

REVENGE OF THE NERVES

WHAT IS THE BEST WAY TO HANDLE NERVES?

It makes sense to be nervous before giving a presentation. After all, most people give boring presentations; why should you be better than most? Okay, I know that sounds depressing, but I'm just being realistic. It actually is quite rational to be nervous before a presentation. But the main reason that most people get these kinds of jitters is a fear of the unknown. If you haven't actually seen yourself give your presentation, then you don't know what you are presenting to the outside world. After all, a presentation is not what is on a PowerPoint slide or a chart; it's you standing or sitting in front of people and talking. If you haven't seen yourself on video giving your talk, then the rough draft of your presentation is the one you give to your final, intended audience. And since rough drafts are—by definition—rough, it makes sense to be nervous if you are going to wing it in front of people.

HOW DO I DEAL WITH PRESPEECH JITTERS?

If I were coaching you to become a world-class, spell-binding orator, I would advise you to rehearse for days and days, and watch dozens of video rehearsals. But I want to make your life easier and save you time, so all you have to do is rehearse on video until you've seen yourself give a pretty good presentation. It doesn't have to be perfect; you don't have to generate a standing ovation, and you don't have to reduce your ums and uhs to zero. You just have to be pretty good compared to all of the other people to whom your bosses and colleagues compare you.

How do you know if you are pretty good? Just watch the video of yourself practicing. If you think you are pretty good, then you probably are. Great! Now you are good to go. But if you think you are incredibly boring, monotone, and tedious or confusing, then you are also probably right. So practice your presentation again on video. This time, do less of the stuff you don't like and more of the stuff you do like. Now, review the video again.

For a very high percentage of people—and I hope you are one of them—two video rehearsals will often be enough. **Warning:** the first time you watch yourself practice the speech, you will hate it. Spend a few minutes tweaking your outline, and then do the speech again on video. Watch it. Now, you are likely to see something you can live with. Congratulations, you are now virtually guaranteed to give a pretty good presentation.

7

SUPPLEMENTARY MATERIALS

SHOULD I SEND ADVANCE MATERIALS?

Here is the reason *not* to send materials to people in advance of a presentation: "If I send them all of my content, they won't need me, they won't be impressed by me, they will be ready to poke holes in my data, and they will have ammunition to use against me. Better to keep them in the dark!!!"

That's the reason I use here, but it's just not a good reason.

WHAT SHOULD I SEND, AND HOW?

I want you to give a pretty good presentation—really, I do. *And* I want you to be lazy. The more content you give your audience in advance, the more they will be familiar with your ideas, and the easier it will be for them to grasp what you're saying during your speech. All of this works to your advantage.

Now, you might be thinking, "But my group is too lazy; they will never read any of the advance materials!" Well, that's all the better. Now your audience has seen you send stuff, and they feel guilty for not reading it. You get credit for being thorough, and they are on the defensive; either way, you win.

HOW FAR IN ADVANCE AND TO WHOM?

I think you should send out as much info as possible the moment you have a booking on the calendar for your presentation—even if it's months away. Then send something out again a few days before—even if it's the same content.

The final fear people have is that audiences will complain if the same material is covered in the speech that is covered in the text. Relax; this will not happen. As long as you don't read the PowerPoint (and you would never do that, right?), then there is no danger of most people even realizing your content is the same. So dump your data on your audience in advance; just don't do a boring data dump in the middle of your speech.

8

PRACTICE MAKES PERFECT

SHOULD I REHEARSE? HOW FAR IN ADVANCE?

The best way to rehearse is to start as far in advance as possible. But since you just need your speech to be pretty good—not world class—I will cut you some slack. Don't bother rehearsing until the day before the speech is due. And you don't have to practice in front of a mirror (that will only make you paranoid about your nose or your hair). Instead, all you need to do is rehearse once in front of a tiny video camera, either a cell phone camera or webcam.

HOW AND TO WHOM CAN I REHEARSE?

After you have recorded your speech, watch it. I know you don't want to do this, but it really is essential if you want to give a pretty good speech and avoid giving a pretty awful speech. If you watch a video of your speech and you feel it's pretty awful, chances are that you're right—it *is* awful! That's okay, just try again (on video) and do less of the stuff you don't like and do more of the stuff you do like. Just keep on doing this until you can watch a speech of yourself and conclude that it's pretty good. You don't have to make it fantastic or perfect—just pretty good. This might require just one recording, or it might require four. Regardless, this is a quick and easy process. People who make awful, boring speeches never rehearse on video. They might think about it; they might even contemplate it for hours; but they never actually record themselves because they are too chicken.

It's okay to be scared, but preferably, you should be more scared of giving a lousy speech.

The number one rule for giving a pretty good speech is to rehearse on video *at least once,* and then watch and critique yourself.

9

YOUR APPEARANCE

WHAT KEY RULES SHOULD I FOLLOW?

Of course, you want to give some thought to your appearance when you are preparing to give a presentation. There are two main factors to think about:

1. Is my appearance **consistent** with the message I am trying to convey?
2. Is there anything I'm wearing that could **distract** my audience from focusing on my message?

In terms of the first point, if you are a financial manager who's attempting to get a major foundation to invest $100 million with you, then you obviously want to wear an extremely expensive and conservative suit, perhaps blue. You want to look established, not flashy, and as if you are already successful and don't need their money. However, if you are an artist who is trying to convey your own brand of quirky creativity, then wearing a blue business suit would be the worst thing you could wear. What you wear needs to communicate who you are and what you are about as much as your words do.

When it comes to number two, you want to make sure that every single element of your appearance is in sync. If you are a businessperson asking people to invest money with you and you have a conservative suit, shirt, and shoes but a Grateful Dead Jerry Garcia tie on, then your audience members are likely to be confused and scratching their heads with distractions.

One important appearance rule: Look at yourself in a mirror before you start to present. Perform one last check to see if your hair is sticking up, if there is any lipstick smudged on or spinach stuck in your teeth. This can help avoid all sorts of appearance blunders.

The only other rule you should follow is to dress at the same level as—or one notch above—your audience members. If your audience is wearing sports jackets, you might want to wear a suit. But don't dress *two* notches above. If, for example, you are addressing a tech audience in which everyone is wearing jeans and a T-shirt and you show up in a suit to present to them, they may look at you as though you are a total loser. Always factor in the image you want for yourself, the expectations the audience has for you, and the need to avoid distraction. Focus on those three things, and your appearance will be fine.

Bonus tip: If you are giving a presentation in front of more than a couple of people and you will be standing, ask a friend or colleague to give you a thorough once-over from front to back. Nothing is worse than finishing a presentation and realizing that the back of your jacket or skirt was accidently tucked into the top of your pants or underwear.

IS THERE ANYTHING TO BE CAREFUL TO AVOID?

It is true that there are a lot more pitfalls for women giving a presentation when it comes to their appearance. Like it or not, it is a reality that a man can spend two minutes shaving, 30 seconds combing his hair (if he has any), and then throw on a classically tailored suit and shirt that he's had for seven years, and he is good to go. No audience will think twice about his appearance. But since there are infinitely more fashion choices for women—everything from clothes to jewelry to makeup—there are more judgments your audience, both women and men, will make.

Here are a few mistakes that often get female presenters into trouble:

- **Hair.** Make sure your hair doesn't obscure your eyes or require touching when you are giving a presentation. If you constantly have to brush your hair back behind your ears while you speak, there is the very real problem that this can seem sexually alluring to some in your audience. If nothing else, it can be distracting and seem unprofessional. While there are certain chic hairstyles that have the bangs going over the eyebrows and touching the eyes, this can be very distracting for audience members if they can't see your eyes; so try to wear a hairstyle that doesn't get in your way.
- **Sex appeal.** While showing cleavage and leg is almost always a surefire way to get attention, this is likely to detract from attention to the ideas in your presentation. For most women in most industries most of the time, it is better to strive to be attractive without overtly showcasing sex appeal.
- **Shoes.** By all means, wear shoes that you like and are proud of. However, if you are giving a presentation that requires you to stand—especially for longer than five minutes—make sure you are wearing shoes that are comfortable (or at least don't cause enough pain to make you wince). And whatever you do, don't wear a brand **new** pair of shoes for the first time during a walking or standing presentation.

- **Makeup.** Try to be understated here. Makeup that might be considered normal or appropriate in Los Angeles, Miami, or New York City might be considered *way* too much if you are giving a breakfast presentation to a commodities trade group in Kansas City. Additionally, if you wear bright lipstick or blush on your cheeks and you are being projected on a video screen while speaking at a large conference hall, the camera and lights can make your makeup appear even more prominent—even cartoonish.
- **Jewelry.** Big earrings and big/multiple bracelets will attract lots of attention; so if that's what you want, fine. Otherwise, wear smaller and less jewelry than usual—unless, of course, you are a jewelry designer and want to attract attention to designs.

Part Two

THE
PRESENTATION

10

VISUAL AIDS

WHEN SHOULD I USE VISUAL AIDS?

The only time to use visual aids is when you have something visual that will increase the odds of your audience understanding and remembering your message.

WHAT TYPES SHOULD I USE?

If you want to give a pretty good presentation, please keep the following principles about various visual aids in mind:

- **Video.** Don't bother! This has the potential to add lots of headaches. I use video every day because I am a professional speaker; I have to show video of people speaking, and they pay me lots of money to do so. But I'm assuming that you *aren't* a professional speaker so I recommend that you stay as far away from video as possible. There are a million things that can go wrong, and dealing with them can become a black hole that sucks up your time. Stay away—you won't be sorry!
- **PowerPoint.** Don't use PowerPoint just because everyone else is; but do use it if you feel you have some visuals (i.e., graphics, photos, charts, or images) that will help your audience understand your ideas better. *Never* use PowerPoint to simply display bullet points with words on it.
- **Emails/memos/handouts.** If you've got a lot of text on the subject you are presenting, give it to your audience in every way possible. Email them

everything you've written. Give a handout after your presentation. But don't feel the need to read to people a text memo that you have cut and pasted into a PowerPoint.

- **Flip charts/whiteboards.** These are great for drawing something that can be more easily grasped in a visual manner. Drawing on a chart or board is also helpful; it slows you down to a point that prompts you to discuss only one topic at a time.

- **Props.** Actual props are a great way of making your ideas come alive to an audience. So, for example, if you are talking about the problems of a deep freeze destroying an orange crop, don't just show a Power-Point photo of a damaged orange. Instead, simply pass around a damaged orange for each person in the room to touch. This doesn't work for large audiences, but for the average business audience of 30 people or fewer, props are an excellent and underused way of making your points more memorable.

- **Cheat sheets.** This is actually the most important visual aid of all: a one-page cheat sheet just for *you* to consult during your presentation. This page of notes should have one to three words per bullet point to trigger your memory, plus any key numbers or facts that you might not easily remember. Make this cheat sheet your best friend; and make multiple copies to place in different parts of the room if you plan on presenting while standing.

Finally, remember that no matter what presentation tools you use, it is essential that you practice at least once in circumstances similar to the one where you will be giving your presentation. Slides that look great on your laptop will look fuzzy and hard to read on a projected screen. A PowerPoint slide playing off of a DVD on your laptop suddenly doesn't play at all when the conference organizer tells you that the computer being used in front of the audience has no DVD drive and there is no time to change computers.

Key concept: You don't want to *ever* have to learn or become familiar with a new tool, trick, prop, or piece of equipment in front of an audience. Do that in private, so that you look comfortable when it comes time to present.

11

STAGE PRESENCE

How Should I Use the Stage?

SHOULD I WALK OUT INTO THE AUDIENCE?

If you want to become a professional motivational speaker and create a true theatrical experience for your audience every time you speak, then you may wish to hire a small army of acting, voice, and dance coaches to choreograph your every move on the platform. But if you just want to give a pretty good presentation, you can forget all of that nonsense. Instead, just focus on doing one thing: *move.*

I know that sounds simple, and almost overly simplistic. But most awful presenters and mediocre speakers freeze up. They stand behind a lectern and lean on it as if it were a life preserver. They hold their hands in the fig leaf position or the military position, or they put them in their pockets (doing who knows what!).

All you have to do to distinguish yourself from the pack of awful speakers is to move around a little. It's basically walking and talking; something you have done since you were in kindergarten. I know that giving presentations probably isn't your idea of fun; it fact, it makes most people a little uncomfortable. And because of that, your natural inclination is to freeze like a rabbit trying to blend into the weeds.

Unfortunately, you won't blend in this way. So I want to make it really easy for you. Don't worry about making big, sweeping gestures with your arms. Forget about getting down on one knee to act out some drama in your life. Instead, imagine yourself in a three-by-three-foot box on the floor. Try to walk around and cover all four corners of the box from time to time as you speak. All this really means is taking a step or two in any direction. This doesn't seem like much; but given that most nervous speakers look and act liked potted plants, you will come across as more comfortable, confident, and relaxed than most speakers. (Even if you're not!)

If you are standing behind a lectern, that's okay; but don't lean on it or touch it. And since you are moving around in an imaginary three-foot box, you will occasionally step far enough away from the lectern so that your audience can see your whole body. Great! This makes you look much more courageous and confident than most uncomfortable speakers.

SHOULD I USE HAND MOVEMENTS?

You certainly don't want to be seen as fidgeting in front of a crowd; but the opposite of fidgeting is not to be frozen. Instead, you want to move in the way you normally do when you are talking to a friend you like. Your face, hands, shoulders, torso, and even your eyebrows *move*. The good news is that you don't have to go to acting school for any of this. You just have to move the way you normally do.

I truly believe that if we could transfer the billions of hours wasted each year by people obsessing over what to do with their hands during a presentation, then we could solve both the world hunger and energy crises. For the most part, worrying about what to do with your hands is a waste of time.

Through the research I've done by working with clients from six continents, I can tell you categorically that audiences around the world respond most favorably to speakers who *gesture* throughout their whole presentation. I can also tell you that, without a doubt, when presenters watch video of themselves presenting, they are frequently flabbergasted and appalled that they move their hands when they speak (even though everyone else in the room thought the hand movement looked great.)

If I were trying to help you become a world-class speaker or a top-tier presidential candidate, I would videotape you extensively in order to get you to move your hands in ways that look natural. But you don't have to worry about any of this!

If your goal is to give a pretty good presentation, then it doesn't matter if you move your hands or not; so you can just take this off of your list of things to worry about. Yes, it is always best if you can move your hands and gesture normally when giving your presentation. But if you keep your hands frozen or flat on a table or lectern— or holding a laser—that's okay, too, as long as you have something interesting and useful to say in your presentation.

There's only one thing you don't want to do with your hands when giving a presentation: fidget, rub your hands together nervously, play with your rings, or do anything else that suggests you are incredibly nervous—because that's what most of the other presenters in the room are going to do. As long as you don't make their mistake, you will stand out as pretty good in comparison.

WHERE SHOULD I LOOK?

Facial expressions can be tricky, and many presenters rack their brains thinking of what kinds of facial expressions to make, when to make them, and in whose direction.

There are three kinds of eye contact that presenters can have with audiences:

1. Staring at the floor, reading notes or staring at the PowerPoint slides—near zero percent eye contact with audience. (This is obviously what the worst speakers do.)
2. Scanning the audience like a windshield wiper, maybe a fast one or a slow one.
3. Giving each individual in the audience personal eye contact for a full thought, about six seconds or so. (World-class professional speakers like Bill Clinton do this.)

If you do the first, you won't be a pretty good presenter—you will be flat-out awful.

If you try to do number three, you will likely get flustered and frustrated.

So, my recommendation is that you try number two, and just look around the room. You can scan it quickly or slowly—the slower the better. If you can lock eyes with a few people around the room, so much the better. Try to look at every part of the room. If you ignore any one part of the room, that part of the room will ignore you back.

The main issue you have to decide is: are you going to ignore the people in the room or are you going to look at people? If you look at people, they will look back at you; and this will increase the chance that you'll give a pretty good presentation. If you don't look at people, then there is a good chance that they will, in turn, ignore you; and there is a *great* chance that you will give an awful presentation. It really is that simple.

It's okay to look at notes from time to time, especially if you can do it in conjunction with picking up a glass of water, putting down a glass of water, or appearing to push the advance button on your projector.

Finally, think about your facial expressions. Boring, awful presenters have a blank look on their faces. Good presenters are expressive; they show when they are excited, happy, sad, or disappointed. You are not supposed to start "acting" expressive because, unless you are a professional actor, this is likely to look and sound phony. The challenge is to be comfortable enough with your material so that you can actually think and talk "in the moment" rather than nervously fixate on what you are going to say five seconds from now. If you are fixated on what you are going to say, as if you were reading off of a teleprompter in your brain, then you will lose all expressiveness from your face.

A final word: many people worry about being too expressive with their face or mouth. *This is not a problem.* Don't worry about being too expressive. Instead, worry about looking as flat as George Washington on a dollar bill. Move your face and show your emotions when you speak. Then, even if you make mistakes from time to time, you will still give a pretty good presentation.

12

Damned if You Do, Damned if You Don't

SHOULD I READ OR MEMORIZE MY PRESENTATION?

Reading a presentation versus memorizing a presentation—talk about a scenario where you are damned if you do and damned if you don't! Both options are horrible. Let's take a look at the reading option. At first blush, reading seems easy. After all, you've been reading your whole life. If you get nervous, all of your words are in front of you, so it seems like this is the safest route, right? Wrong!

Reading a presentation in front of people is the absolute dumbest thing you could ever do if your goal is to give a pretty good presentation because, unless you have been a news anchor and reading a script for three hours a day for the last 20 years, you are going to be terrible. Why? When you read, you break your eye contact with your audience; you become flat, monotone, and boring; and you speak at the same speed.

Please keep in mind that reading a speech is really hard work. Even a master like former President Ronald Reagan would practice his State of the Union speech three hours a night for a week, and then still spend an entire day doing videotaped rehearsal, all so he didn't seem like he was reading a speech! I really don't think you want to spend the time it takes to get good at reading a speech. And if you don't spend all of that time, you will be awful and fall way short of your goal of being pretty good. So what's the next option?

You could try to memorize your speech. Yea, right. In case you have forgotten middle school vocabulary tests or high school Spanish, memorizing stuff is *really hard*. Even if you're good at memorizing words for a test, that doesn't mean you are going to be able to recall information when you add in the tension associated with having to speak while a bunch of people are staring at you. Worst of all, even if you *did* successfully memorize your presentation, there is a great chance that you would sound canned, phony, flat, and robotic and memorized when people heard you. Yuck! No one would want to listen to you. There is a reason that Meryl Streep makes the big bucks. Acting is really hard if you do it in such a way that it doesn't seem like you are obviously acting.

Take my word for it: you don't want to memorize anything. It's too difficult and fraught with peril.

So what's the solution?

HOW CAN I MAKE NOTES AND USE THEM PROPERLY?

I recommend that you work off of a single page of notes when you speak. Use a simple outline, one with bullet points instead of full sentences. Each bullet point should have no more than three or four words attached to it, just enough to jog your memory on what you want to say on that point. Make your words in a really big font so that you don't have to bend over to read them, pick up the paper, or put on your glasses. Put every key point, number, fact, and story title that are absolutely essential on your paper; but only the stuff that is completely necessary. If you can't fit it all on one page while using large type, then you have a problem.

The key factor here is to spend most of your time looking at your audience while you present. You'll occasionally have to look down at your notes to figure out what to say next, but you shouldn't have enough text to keep your head buried for very long.

People often describe what I am advocating here as ad-libbing or being extemporaneous, but this is not quite right. It would be truly hard to just "think on the spot" while you're standing up there in front of people; and I don't want to make you work that hard. I'm simply advocating that you follow a road map. You've already thought about what you want to say. You've practiced on video once or twice. You have notes. You glance at the first bullet point. You look up and talk about it for a minute or two, using comfortable conversational language you've used before. You aren't saying it word for word the same as you did in rehearsal because you aren't trying to memorize anything—and anyway, it's not important to say it word for word. When you finish one point and said everything you have to say, then you simply stop talking for a second. Without embarrassment, you look down at your notes, see what the next bullet point is, then look up at your audience and start talking again. Repeat the process until you have finished the speech.

If you remember the days before GPS devices told us every turn to make while driving, you may recall actually having to use a large, paper map. Maps were great to plot out a trip before you started driving a car, and they were helpful if you occasionally had to glance down at them while at a stop light. But if you kept your eyes focused on a map the entire time you were driving, you would likely drive head-on into another car and kill yourself, or at least make everyone else in the car with you crazy. The same is true when you try to keep your eyes on your notes the whole time when giving a presentation.

A few other notes about notes:
- Always bring at least two copies.
- Never use handwritten notes.
- Limit your notes to one page.
- Don't read your notes out loud at the same time you are reading. Instead, glance down, scoop up the words, then look up, then speak.
- Always remember to relax. You don't have to worry about forgetting anything—your notes are right in front of you.

13

TESTING . . . 1, 2, 3 . . .

SHOULD I USE A MICROPHONE?

There are only two reasons to *ever* use technology when giving a presentation:

1. It makes it easier for your audience to understand or remember your key points.
2. It makes it easier to accomplish your goal of making your audience understand and remember your key points.

Please note your relative order of importance: you come second to the audience. Why is it important to point this out? Because quite often inexperienced and average speakers will say things like, "I don't need a microphone." Well, obviously, the speaker *never* needs a microphone to speak. But some of your audience members may need you to talk into a microphone that is then amplified into a speaker if they are going to *hear you*. Unless you are talking to two people sitting right in front of you, you can never be certain if people need you to use a microphone or not.

WHEN AND HOW SHOULD I USE A MICROPHONE?

I actually take my own wireless microphone with me wherever I go to speak; and I recommend that all professional speakers do so. But you don't have to. Let's keep things simple. My recommendation is to simply use a microphone anytime you are in a room that has one or someone offers one to you. Of course, if you are in a room that holds 500 people but you are speaking to only five people, then you don't want to be far away from the people on a stage just to get close to a microphone. In that case, you would just get as close as possible to the five people and speak.

WHAT SHOULD I DO IF SOMETHING BREAKS OR MALFUNCTIONS DURING MY PRESENTATION?

Here are some general rules you need to follow when using technology with a presentation:

- Assume the worst.
- Practice using the technology in advance. That includes the laptop, microphone, projector, speaker, laser, and anything that you are going to use in front of people.
- Practice in the same environment as you will be giving your final presentation; that is, if you are presenting to 400 people in a conference hall using a big projector, then practice in that hall or one that is similar. Don't simply practice on your laptop in a hotel room because it's easy to do anything with your laptop in a hotel room, and this will give you a false sense of confidence.
- When microphones break and computers freeze, don't panic and don't complain. If there is a tech person around, calmly mention that your microphone is no longer working and ask for help. If your computer freezes, calmly restart it without drawing attention to your problems.

- Have a Plan B. If your PowerPoint stops working, just be ready to talk to people using nothing more than your paper notes.
- Test all technology either right before you speak (if possible) or during the largest break of the day (breakfast, lunch, or dinner) preceding your presentation so that you can make sure you know how everything works.
- If you get lots of feedback from a microphone, just stop talking and step back. This solves most problems right away.
- Never, ever try to *learn* any piece of technology in front of people. Every laptop keyboard and every remote control are slightly different. It's really tough to learn anything new when you have the added tension associated with being in front of people who are all staring at you.
- If you are going to use PowerPoint with video clips and use a microphone, give yourself an extra hour to rehearse in the room where you will be presenting— because there are a million things that can go wrong.
- Never forget that the presentation is about the ideas you have to help, inform, inspire, and educate your audience. The presentation is not about your technology.

14

AUDIENCE PARTICIPATION

HOW SHOULD I ENCOURAGE THE AUDIENCE TO PARTICIPATE (IF AT ALL?)

You are probably wondering, "Why would I want to engage the audience? That sounds scary! I'd like my audience to sit there and shut up, so I can finish and get the heck out of there!"

I sympathize with you—I really do. But I also want to make your life as easy as possible and to increase your odds of being perceived as a pretty good presenter. One of the biggest dangers we have to worry about as speakers is that our audience gets bored, zones out, and then remembers us as awful speakers. This is a failure for us.

But if you engage your audience, they won't be bored; and engagement means two-way communication. You've probably had an interesting conversation with a friend, spouse, or family member that lasted all day; not necessarily because anyone said anything brilliant, but because there was a back-and-forth engagement that allowed you to talk—so it wasn't boring.

When people say they don't like to be "lectured to," they typically mean that they don't like one-way communication where one person does all of the talking, and they have to just sit there and take it. This is why everything you do in your presentation needs to *not* remind people of a lecture. You want to talk to, have a conversation with, and engage people.

Here are some simple tips to help you engage your audience:

- Ask people questions when you are presenting.
- Encourage people to ask you questions at *any time*—not just at the end of your presentation.
- Look at audience members to see if they understand what you are saying. If they look confused, stop and ask them where you've lost them.
- Encourage people to disagree with you and give other opinions—not just ask you questions.
- Engage audience members not just with your words, but with your eyes, focus, and smile as well.

I know there is a part of you saying, "I don't want people interrupting me during my presentation! They will disrupt my train of thought. I'll forget what I'm going to say. Can't they just shut up until I finish?"

You *could* do it this way, but you pay a real price, and there is very little upside. If you let listeners interrupt you with questions during your presentation, you often end up with a better outcome—because the questioner may be pointing out a place where you were unclear or fuzzy. The other great value of letting someone ask a question is that it creates a variety of voices in the room, which makes your presentation more interesting.

And yes, it's true; people like the sound of their own voice. It might seem odd, but people will say nicer things about your presentation because you let them talk a little and you listened to them. I understand your concern that allowing audience members to interrupt you at any time will make you forget what you are going to say, freeze, panic, develop flop sweat, and then have a heart attack and die. Fortunately, you don't have to ever worry about remembering what to say because—as you recall from an earlier chapter—you have a simple text outline in front of you. Since you can glance at this at any time, you never have to burden yourself with memorizing stuff. This takes all the pressure off.

IS THE TRADITIONAL "SAVING QUESTIONS FOR THE END" METHOD REALLY THE BEST OPTION OR JUST THE MOST COMMONLY USED?

So, you are probably asking yourself, why is it so common for people to hold all questions until the end of a presentation? Two reasons:

1. If someone is addressing a large audience of 100 or even thousands of people, it is too unwieldy to take questions throughout. I assume that the vast majority of the time, you are speaking to small audiences, so this does not apply to you.
2. People hold questions until the end because they are scared. This is a reason, but it's not a good reason.

If you take questions throughout your presentation, you will score lots of points with your audience and seem better than most presenters. You will be making some favorable deposits in the credit department. This means that if you do mess up in part of your speech, or are less than riveting in other parts, you will have some goodwill stored up. The result is that even if you have some gaps and stumbles in parts of your presentation, the strengths of being engaging will outweigh those, and your overall presentation performance will be judged as pretty good.

15

TIMING IS EVERYTHING

What Do I Do if My Presentation is Running Short or Long?

RUNNING SHORT

Running short is usually not a problem. Sure, if you have been paid $50,000 to give a keynote speech in front of 5,000 people and you are supposed to speak for an hour and are done after 10 minutes, then you have a problem on your hands. But I'm assuming—since you simply want to give a pretty good presentation—that you aren't in the professional speaking business. Great! That takes all the pressure off.

It's highly unlikely that, if you've been allotted 30 minutes and finish after 20, anyone in your audience is going to be upset with you; in fact, you are likely to be proclaimed a hero! If you have covered your main points and done so in a memorable way, then sit down. Don't worry about running a little short.

However, sometimes people run short because they race through their speech in order to finish faster and sit down. *This* is a problem. Occasionally, people finish earlier than their allotted time because they strip the speech of all interesting examples, stories, case studies, and vignettes. This, too, is a problem.

Your goal should not be to give a presentation in as brief amount a time as possible or to finish in less than the time allotted. Instead, you want to communicate a few important ideas that you care about and that you want the audience to care about. If you do that, the time will often take care of itself.

If you are allotted 30 minutes to speak and you finish after 90 seconds, then that obviously suggests a problem. Either you rushed too much, or you completely forgot entire sections of your presentation. If you rehearse on video—something you've already pledged to do just once in order to give a pretty good presentation—then you should already know how long your speech lasts. This way, there should be no surprises about coming up short.

Finally, remember that you will never hear anyone say the following: "Wow! That speaker was interesting, memorable, relevant, and gave me a lot of good ideas I can use in my business, but I sure am disappointed that she spoke for 10 minutes less than scheduled."

RUNNING LONG

For starters, don't panic! Next, don't waste time apologizing for going long because the time you spend talking about going long is actually making you go even longer.

Going long can be a function of several complex factors: Did you start late? Did you plan poorly and have way too much information? Did you get sidetracked? Was the audience so fascinated with you that they bombarded you with questions?

Here are two other factors you need to take into consideration:

1. **What are the other time commitments for your audience?** It's one thing if you're speaking to your own employees and you are running five minutes late for a meeting that is supposed to end at 9:30 AM. If you are the last speaker of a five-day conference and you were supposed to finish at

4:00 PM and everyone has 6:00 PM flights—and you are still talking at a quarter till 5:00—then you have a huge, HUGE problem.

2. **Are people engaged with you?** If they are fascinated, hanging on your every word, and are on the edge of their seats, then don't worry if you are a few minutes long.

There are two main reasons for running long. The first is that you started very late through no fault of your own. What I recommend you do is ask the coordinator of the meeting how long they want you to speak. There are three choices:

1. Speak for the allotted time you originally had—say, 30 minutes—even if that means you finish at 11:20 and not 11:00 as originally scheduled.
2. Finish at the originally scheduled time, no matter what. So if you were supposed to start at 10:30 AM and finish at 11:00, and you don't start until 10:50, you would then say everything you need to in 10 minutes, thus finishing by 11:00.
3. The final option is to compromise somewhat, say, giving you 20 minutes so that you still finish 10 minutes later than scheduled but only have to shrink your presentation by one third.

Here's the only secret you need to know in order to appear to be a pretty good presenter: don't act like you are bothered in the *least* by the time change. Most speakers look and act nervous if there is a change. They apologize for starting or finishing late; they pull on their shirt and tie like Rodney Dangerfield. Don't do any of this. Instead, focus on delivering the most important material you had for the crowd in the amount of time you have (as defined by the person in charge, even if that is you). Don't act stressed or rushed—even if you are.

I realize that what I am telling you to do might seem difficult, but it's actually easier than the approach that most presenters take in these situations. When they realize that they are running late, they start to panic. Next, they start to talk faster and faster, thus destroying the audience's ability to understand them. Then, they eliminate all of their interesting stories and examples in order to get to all of the facts, thus ensuring that nothing will be remembered. And to top it all off, they waste time talking *about* time, which is always a completely useless thing to do.

So don't do any of these things. If you've prepared five main points that will take 25 minutes to cover and are suddenly told to finish in 15 minutes, then just cover your first three points—complete with examples and stories. Then let people know that you can send them a memo or other documentation to go over the stuff you didn't have time for if they want more information.

Here is another simple and easy technique. Let's say you have concluded your presentation, but there are a lot of questions. You feel torn; on the one hand, you want to finish on time and you can see that half of the room is anxious and itching to get out of there. On the other hand, half of the room is riveted by what you are saying and has a genuine interest in asking you relevant questions that you could answer in your presentation—and you don't want to disappoint them.

A simple solution is to announce the following: "I know that some of you have to leave, so we are going to conclude as scheduled right now at 1:00 PM. For those of you who have more questions or would like to chat more about this subject, I would be happy to resume the conversation in two minutes right here—immediately after we let our colleagues get by who have to leave." This way, you look like a class act; everybody wins and gets what they want. The people who want to leave don't feel awkward or embarrassed about having to sneak out or step over people, and the people who wanted more content from you will get it. *And* you appeared to be a pretty good presenter in the process.

Another tip when it comes to avoiding the problem of running long is to time your rehearsal the right way. Most people make the mistake of reading their presentation silently, and then timing it with a stopwatch. They don't take into account that it takes a lot longer to talk to people, pause, walk around, and take questions. What might take you only 5 minutes to read out loud might take you 10 minutes to say in front of people. And then, if you factor in a question or two, it could add another 50 percent. My recommendation is to time your rehearsal, and then add at least another 20 percent to get a sense of how long it will take in the real world.

Final tip: Always have a clock, watch, or some time-piece clearly in your view when giving a presentation. You don't want to have to be worrying about going long in the middle of your presentation and not really knowing what time it is. I just take my watch off and put it on the table or lectern in front of me; that way, no one has to notice me making a furtive glance at my wrist.

16

DON'T PANIC

What Should I Do if My Mind Goes Blank Halfway Through My Presentation?

It is inevitable that you will get nervous and your mind will go blank from time to time when you give presentations. However, it's not inevitable that you'll have a bad reaction to your mind going blank, start to panic, tell people your mind has gone blank, faint, or run out of the room crying like a little baby!

None of these things will happen to you because you are going to cheat (in an ethical manner, of course). If you follow the techniques I have advocated, then you will never give a presentation without having an outline telling you where you are going at all times. The outline will be in big bold letters, and with no more than three or four words on each line. It will be simple, clear, and easy to follow.

Why do you need this? Imagine you are driving down Interstate 95 and you zone out and daydream for a few minutes. All of a sudden, you see exit 77; and you don't panic if you have a clear set of written instructions next to you in the front seat. (Let's assume your global positioning system [GPS] is in the shop.) If your directions say you aren't supposed to get off until exit 59, and you notice that the numbers are still going down, then you realize that you are going in the right direction; you understand that you aren't lost; and you aren't worried about where you are exactly at that moment. You know more or less where you are relative to where you were and where you are going. You don't break out in a cold sweat in the car because you simply feel no pressure. In fact, you aren't worried about being lost, and you didn't even bother to memorize the directions because you correctly deduced that you didn't need to. The directions are right next to you and available at a quick glance at any time. You feel particularly confident because— unlike the satellite on a GPS failing or the power cord disconnecting—the paper on which your driving instructions are written will never fail you (unless you spill coffee on them).

All of this is exactly the same when you have written notes in front of you for the presentation you are giving. You can now just enjoy the journey of the drive, so to speak. The whole concept of your memory freezing becomes less relevant because you aren't forcing it to do some difficult and unnatural task in the first place.

Remember, your goal is to give a pretty good presentation, not give a Broadway-worthy performance to be cast in the next David Mamet play. Don't force yourself to memorize and deliver lines flawlessly because that's really hard to do. Have more modest goals of talking around a set of notes. You will be 100 percent successful at delivering a pretty good presentation—and then some.

17

TECHNICAL DIFFICULTIES

WHAT DO I DO IF I ENCOUNTER TECHNICAL DIFFICULTIES DURING MY PRESENTATION?

The first thing you want to do when you encounter a technical problem while presenting is *not* to look or sound panicked. I realize that asking you to do this seems hard, since it's the time when you are most panicked. However, I am actually telling you it's okay to *feel* panicked—just don't tell or show anyone. For example, one day I was giving a PowerPoint presentation and I had forgotten to plug my computer in to charge the battery. Since this was an all-day training presentation, the computer went dead in the middle of one of my presentations.

I could have blurted out, "Oh my God, I'm a fool! I forgot to plug in my power cord!"

But I didn't. Inwardly, I'm saying a Homer Simpson "Doh!" to myself and wanting to slap my hand to my forehead. But outwardly, I continued talking about the subject at hand. Then I threw a question to an audience member. While he was talking, I quickly opened my computer bag, pulled out my power cord, plugged in the computer, turned it on, and hoped the PowerPoint presentation would come back alive in a couple of minutes. It did! And no one in my audience had any idea there had ever been a problem.

Here are the fundamental rules when it comes to tech problems during a presentation:

- Don't panic.
- Don't tell anyone if you can solve the problem yourself.
- Don't tell anyone if the problem can be skipped over without anyone's really being bothered or noticing— say, a PowerPoint slide that has just gone blank.
- If you are in a facility that has a tech support person and you have a problem that entails something like a microphone going dead, then calmly ask for the tech person to come help you.
- If you get audio feedback when you move to a certain area, then avoid that area.
- At all times, be prepared to finish your presentation without using any one piece of technology—whether it's a projector, speaker, or laptop.

HOW CAN I AVOID TECH ISSUES IN THE FIRST PLACE?

Here are the top nine rules to use if your goal is to avoid technology problems in the first place:

1. Don't use video in your presentation unless it is *absolutely necessary.*
2. Multimedia means multi-headaches, so don't use unless you are willing to rehearse numerous times in the final circumstances of your presentation.
3. Rehearse on the actual pieces of technology you will be using; that is, don't practice on your laptop in a hotel room and then give the presentation at a hotel conference room the next day using someone else's laptop and remote clicker. Practice on the actual tech stuff you're going to use.

4. Laptops freeze, so prepare for it. Get ready to restart in the middle of a presentation.
5. Bring a backup of any technology you use. That means an extra projector, bulbs, laptop, video cameras, and so on. You can't have too much redundancy.
6. Bring extra batteries for *everything*.
7. Never use a timed PowerPoint presentation unless it is meant to be used independently from your speaking.
8. Unless you are presenting in your own office, make sure you have resolved the whole Mac vs. PC thing in advance. Otherwise, you may not be able to do anything you planned.
9. Keep one very important point in mind: what looks and sounds great on your little laptop may look and sound horrible in a big conference hall. There's different lighting, potentially inferior sound, and different settings on the built-in computer. You must rehearse, rehearse, and rehearse in the final setting if you want to avoid tech problems.

Remember, you aren't giving a PowerPoint speech or a technology speech. You are giving a presentation about ideas; the technology is there simply to enhance your ideas, not the other way around. You are never prepared to give a pretty good presentation unless you can give the presentation without the use of any technology at all.

18

MAY I HAVE YOUR ATTENTION, PLEASE?

WHAT DO I DO IF MY AUDIENCE LOOKS UNINTERESTED?

I don't want you to panic, but this is not good. If you aren't interesting, then you aren't very pretty, or even a little good. You're just plain awful as a presenter.

But you *are* ahead of the game if you even realize that your audience seems uninterested. Most speakers are so focused on their own written text or PowerPoint slides that they wouldn't know if their audience was still in the room—much less paying attention.

Here are the things you *don't* want to do if you sense your audience is losing interest quickly:

- Speak faster to end the ordeal sooner.
- Speak softer so they can't hear how boring you are.
- Look pissed off, as if it's the audience's fault that you are boring.

Instead, let's try to fix the problem—and the problem is what you are saying. There can be a million reasons why your audience is not interested in you. Your subject matter may be too basic or over their heads. Your topic may not match with their interests. You may be the tenth speaker to address the same topic in the last two days at a financial conference. Or you might just remind your audience of the most boring, droning, data-dumping college professor they ever had.

You can try to guess what the problem is, but that's really hard if you aren't clairvoyant (and most of us aren't). Or you can ignore the problem, which only makes it worse. Or you can solve the problem by simply asking an audience member a question or two.

Don't say, "What don't you understand, dummy?" In fact, don't put the onus on your audience members at all. Put it on yourself instead. Say something like, "Tammy, I feel I've been a little unclear. Can you help me figure out where I may have lost the audience?" Now, you look like a class act because you are taking the blame instead of pinning it on others, and audience members will usually be willing and able to give you guidance.

HOW DO I GET THEM BACK?

The easiest way to regain the audience members' interest is to address them by name and ask simple questions:

- "Shane, has that ever happened to you?"
- "Roberta, how have you handled these situations in your business?"
- "Sanjay, are the financial markets affecting the industry as much in your country as they are here in London?"

Audience members for business presentations are no different than people in other social interactions. The more you get your date to talk at dinner, the more charming you will be perceived. So it is with your presentations.

So ask, ask, and ask some more. Most people never get tired of talking about themselves. Of course, you don't have to turn your entire presentation over to your audience members. However, peppering them with a few occasional questions is always a good idea, especially if you feel you are starting to lose them. This works particularly well if you are speaking to a room with 30 people or fewer, with no need for a microphone. However, if you are in a large room with hundreds of audience members, asking questions can be a little more complicated—but not much. As long as you have a handheld microphone, you can randomly ask people questions—as long as you give them a microphone to answer.

While it may seem intimidating to leave the comfort of a lectern, table, or stage if you are speaking in front of hundreds of people, it's easier than you would think to engage an audience. Think of it this way: would you rather do a karaoke solo, or would you prefer to sing with your four best friends so you don't stand out as much? Unless you're an unusually confident singer, you probably prefer the group sing-along. That's essentially what you are doing by asking questions of the audience and letting them share their opinions. Your presentation now becomes a collaborative experience—and that is always more interesting than a solitary lecture.

I have to stress that you don't have to walk around a big auditorium with a microphone à la Oprah Winfrey. You can, as I mentioned before, just stand in one spot. But it is easier than you think to walk around and ask people questions, and you will surely be remembered as a pretty good speaker if you do so.

19

UH . . . UM . . .

How Do I Reduce or Eliminate Nervous Tics Like "Uh" and "Um" in My Speaking?

Everyone says the occasional "um" and "uh," so don't beat yourself up if you do. Bill O'Reilly and Martha Stewart both say "um" and "uh" all the time, and they both make tens of millions of dollars a year just by speaking. So, let's put your problem in perspective. Bill and Martha are still successful because they have messages that audiences find interesting. Your biggest problem is always making sure you have something interesting to say, not whether you have too many ums and uhs.

However, all things considered, the fewer ums and uhs you have cluttering your speech, the better. The first thing you have to do is actually determine if you have the problem. In my experience, executives and salespeople who think they have a problem with too many ums and uhs rarely do; and those who think they don't have a problem are the ones who often *do*.

There is only one way to find out. That's right, let's go to the videotape (or audiotape). Record yourself and then note how often you say "um," "uh," "like," or any other annoying filler words. The video will not lie to you. Keep a tally as you watch it.

Although the occasional verbal tic isn't the end of the world, you do want to pay especially close attention to how many come out of your mouth in the first 30 seconds of your presentation because this is when you are making your first impression. Sadly, the audience will interpret your ums and uhs to mean that you are scared, nervous, and possibly unprepared. It's okay, of course, to be nervous, but we don't want to let our audience know that.

Saying "um" or "uh" is the equivalent of filling up your pauses with punctuation; these sounds are like extra commas. Imagine that someone has sent you a cover letter and a resume. The resume is perfect, but the cover letter has a comma after every word in the first sentence. You could still read and understand the letter; but the extra commas would be both annoying and seriously distracting. That is the problem with too many ums and uhs.

So how do you get rid of these audible fillers? You should not have someone stand in the back of the room and ring a bell every time you say an um or an uh. That will only make you more nervous. You need to re-condition your brain. No, you do not have to hook yourself up to a machine to receive a painful electric shock (this has been suggested to me many times!). I give my clients stickers with the word *um* or *uh* in small type inside a red universal "no" symbol (a circle with a slash through it). Then I place this sticker on my clients' watches, cell phones, computer monitors, or anyplace else where they will see it frequently.

Try it. You look at your watch or cell phone dozens of times a day, and now you get a visual reminder not to say "um" or "uh." After one day, you will still say it, but you will at least be aware of it. After a couple of days, just as you are about to form that sound, the image of "don't say it" pops into your mind. You almost catch it . . . but it still comes out. Drat! But after one week, the image will pop up in your mind and you will be able to hold in the filler word. Now you can simply pause, which will make you sound more comfortable, confident, and authoritative.

I'm happy to send you some free stickers if you send an email to freestickers@tjwalker.com, or you can just create them yourself. Within one week, your audible fillers problem will no longer be a problem.

The goal is not to have zero verbal tics, so don't beat yourself up or wince in the middle of a presentation if one slips out. The solution I've outlined may sound simple, but it really does work—just not instantly. I've used this technique on billionaire fund managers and politicians around the globe, and it works for them. It can work for you, too.

20

Linguistics

What About Accents, Lisps, Stuttering, and Other Distracting Factors?

Don't worry about them. Accents, lisps and stuttering are all problems that can be ignored. Being boring and unmemorable, however, is a problem that needs to be addressed.

In my presentation training practice, I encounter clients from all over the world who believe that their accent or mild speech impediment is a real problem for them and their audiences. However, there just isn't any proof for this theory. Governor Arnold Schwarzenegger's strong Austrian accent didn't hurt his career as an actor or a politician—two professions where speaking is paramount.

Deepak Choprah has an Indian accent, and Dr. Ruth Westheimer has a strong German accent. These two seemed to do okay in their careers, didn't they? Additionally, Winston Churchill, Rudy Giuliani, and John McCain all had some form of a lisp, yet soared to great political heights. Even Jesse Jackson and Joe Biden suffered from stuttering when they were young.

Of course, if you want to be the next Meryl Streep, you need to know how to hide your accent and adapt anyone else's and make it seem natural. But I assume you aren't trying to be the next Meryl Streep—you just want to give a pretty good presentation. To that end, here are the only two questions you need to get right when it comes to dealing with any problems you have regarding accents or speech impediments:

1. Can people hear what you are saying?
2. Can people understand what you are saying?

If the answer to both is yes, then don't worry about these things any longer. If you don't give a pretty good presentation, it won't be because you had an accent or speech impediment; it will be because you gave a boring and unmemorable data dump of a presentation.

The problem for many people with strong regional or foreign accents is that they become self-conscious and try to mask their problem by speaking softer and faster than normal in order to finish sooner. Unfortunately, this combination is deadly—now the presenter cannot be understood at all. Once that happens, you won't even be close to giving a pretty good presentation.

So remember, getting rid of an accent or speech impediment you've had your whole life is hard. Speaking a little louder and slower than normal is pretty easy. Let's stick with the easy approach.

You still might be thinking in the back of your mind that it would be nice to have whatever you consider to be the perfect accent for your audience. Yes, in theory, you can hire an accent reduction coach and go to meet with him once a week for costly and time-consuming accent reduction classes. I don't want to discourage you from personal improvement, but I do want to make life easier for you. Please, take my word for it; we don't all have to sound like NBC anchorman Brian Williams.

It is comparably much easier, faster, and cheaper if you just focus your time and efforts on coming up with something interesting to say to your audience and to give examples and stories. If you do that, your audience is likely to remember what you said—not how you said it. Isn't that your goal?

21

GET TO THE POINT

How Do I Identify Key Points to Reinforce in a Presentation?

Ask. That's the simplest way. You don't have to ask every single person who will be in your audience or spend 100 hours calling people for two months. But you could call one future audience member and ask what he is most interested in, after you provide a menu of your possible messages.

But let's say that won't work because you are giving a presentation to two high-powered investors with whom it took plenty of work just to get the meeting. You can't very well now ask for another half-hour picking either investor's brain before the meeting. In that case, try to find a friend or colleague who has a similar financial perspective and worldview who could give you something close to the perspective of your eventual audience members.

The hard thing to do is spend hundreds of hours doing more research on the Internet and going through colleagues' written reports, and then writing a presentation. The even harder thing is to do all of that and come up with message points that your audience will actually find interesting.

Why not take the easy way out? You can do that just by asking people.

The first step is trying to list all of the important points you want to cover in your presentation. Then, find out from an audience member, or someone who represents your audience, what he is interested in regarding the subject you are addressing. Next, find out which of your messages are also on the list of things that interest your audience. Finally, identify an overlap. If you had 20 key points and your audience was interested in 10 points, but only 5 of their 10 overlap with your points, you now know that you can focus on those 5 points. So relax—the hard part of your speech is done, and you haven't even had to stand up and walk in front of the room yet.

You can have a silvery voice and a commanding stage presence, but if you pick dull or uninteresting messages to communicate to your audience, you will give an awful presentation. However, if you wisely select messages that are important to you *and* your audience, then you can be less than a silver-tongued orator and still give a pretty good presentation.

Most average and below-average presenters never really come up with a good method of selecting the right messages to reinforce in their presentation. And because of that, they just do a data-dump of *all* of their messages. Everything is thrown out, but nothing gets reinforced.

If you actually apply the screens of what you want, what your audience wants, and what you both want, then you have eliminated the temptation of doing a data-dump. You've narrowed your presentation's focus down to a handful of key ideas, and you now have the time and resources to reinforce each point. And the best way to do this is by giving examples, recalling conversations with clients and colleagues, discussing case studies, and even demonstrating.

22

THE Q&A

Should I Conduct a Question-and-Answer Session? If so, How?

Yes, you should *always* give people the option of asking you questions, unless there are strict time restraints that prohibit you from doing so. Most presenters find question-and-answer time easier than delivering a prepared presentation, so you might even find you are more relaxed during this part of your presentation. Audiences also typically enjoy question time more because it allows them the opportunity to participate.

Make no mistake about it: your audience sees your ability to answer questions as a big part of your overall presentation. You need to let people ask you questions, and you need to seem happy about their doing so. Movie stars like Tom Cruise or disgraced politicians can get away with refusing questions, but you can't; so don't even try.

Please keep in mind the following tips regarding Q&A sessions:

- If the audience is fewer than 30 people and there is no hard-and-fast time constriction, encourage people to ask questions at any time during your presentation, not just at the conclusion.
- Listen carefully to each question in its entirety. What you think is the gist of the question might not be once you hear the whole thing.
- Look at the person asking you the question the whole time he or she is asking.
- Begin and end your answer by looking at the person who asked the question. But look at everyone else in

the room during the middle of the answer, so they don't feel left out.

- Limit your answers to a couple of minutes or less; don't give another entire presentation in answer to a question.
- Don't say "good question"—just answer it. (Nobody cares about your opinions on questions, and everyone feels their question was a good one; otherwise, they wouldn't have asked it.)
- If someone starts to give a mini-speech instead of asking a question and you sense others in the audience are getting annoyed, feel free to interrupt after one minute and ask, "Sir (or ma'am), what is the question?"
- If an audience member gives a long-winded rambling series of questions and criticisms that you can tell didn't resonate with the audience, don't feel obligated to give a detailed point-by-point response. Instead, simply look at the audience member and say, "Thanks for sharing that," and move on to the next question.
- If one person asks more than two questions—especially if the questions don't seem interesting to the rest of the crowd—respond this way: "Sir, I'd like to give your concerns the utmost attention they deserve. Because they are complex issues, I'd like to talk to you immediately after the presentation is over so I can address them in more detail. Thanks." Obviously, this doesn't apply if the person asking the question is your boss, a key decision maker, or your number one client.

- There can occasionally be an awkward silence if no one wants to ask the first question, so be prepared by having a question for yourself. You can say, "While you are preparing your questions, let me share with you a question I am frequently asked . . . (then ask yourself a common question, and answer it). This will typically prime the pump for others to ask you questions.
- If you have a hard-and-fast time for finishing the presentation—say, 1:00 PM—and you can tell that half of your audience has to leave right then but the other half still has questions, then I would suggest saying the following: "It's now three minutes till 1:00. I will take one more question now and then we will officially conclude at 1:00, as scheduled, since I know that many of you have to leave then to make your next appointment. But for those who have more questions, please stay; we will be happy to answer questions down here in front once our colleagues have had a chance to leave." Then conclude your Q&A after the "official" ending of your presentation.
- Have fun with question-and-answer time. This is a chance to show people that you are quick on your feet, knowledgeable, and a real person.

23

QUESTIONS FROM THE AUDIENCE

*What if I'm Asked a Question
I Can't Answer?*

Nothing sends chills up the spine of a presenter more than the prospect of giving a presentation and then being asked a question that he or she can't answer. Ugh! The humiliation! The shame! I'll have to resign my position, leave the industry, move to North Korea, and become a subsistence farmer!

Hold on. Don't jump off the cliff just yet. Anytime I give a presentation to a large audience, I'll often ask: Who here can personally remember a time in the past month where you or someone you saw give a presentation failed to answer a question correctly—and it was horribly embarrassing, and everyone knew it? Sure enough, at least 10 percent of the hands go up. So, yes, this is a legitimate concern. But then I'll ask the same audience another question: "How many of you remember seeing someone give a presentation in the past month, and it was so boring you didn't remember a thing the presenter said five minutes after the speech was over?"

This time, about 100 percent of the hands in the room go up. So, if we are going to worry about potential problems, we might as well play the odds and worry about having an interesting presentation in the first place, not the relatively small odds that we can answer a question smoothly.

Nonetheless, at some point in your career, you will be asked a question you can't answer. Here are some things you don't want to do:

- Apologize.
- Laugh nervously.
- Wear an expression on your face that says "oh sh*t!"
- Complain that it's a tough question.
- Look away awkwardly and start fumbling through notes as if the answer will mysteriously appear in front of you.

Here is the little-known secret to giving a pretty good presentation: it is unlikely that people will remember you not knowing the answer to a question. However, it is highly likely that people will remember you not knowing the answer to a question if you appear embarrassed, frustrated, angry, or disappointed. Since many presentations in business and life are somewhat dry and factual in nature, you run the risk of drawing massive attention to your mistakes if they happen to be the only part of your presentation where emotion is displayed.

When asked a question you don't know the answer to, consider the following guidelines:

- Act completely poised, calm, and confident at all times (even when you're not).
- Act genuinely happy to receive the question (especially when you're not).
- If the question is one that is easily obtainable—say, sales figures last quarter broken out by product line for South America—simply reply, "Sally, I will have Jaime send you those sales figures within one hour from now." Stop. Smile. Don't act embarrassed. And act like this is the most obvious and rational way for information like this to be shared. Don't act like

you feel incredibly stupid for not knowing the answer now.

- You might be asked a question to which someone else in the room does know the answer. Don't fumble around awkwardly for minutes, and then sheepishly and meekly ask for help from a colleague. Simply turn as soon as the question is asked, and say something like, "We are fortunate to have Shana, who's an expert on the subject, with us today; I will pose that question to her. . . . " Now you have made the smooth transition to facilitator instead of just the presenter. The audience member gets the information; Shana gets positive public recognition; and in the process, you look like a smooth class act who knows how to bring out the best in a whole team. Everybody wins.

- Occasionally, you may be asked a hypothetical question that is essentially unknowable or something that is knowable to which you just don't know the answer. For example, "If the recession gets worse and unemployment grows to 14 percent by the end of next year, isn't that likely to destroy your company's profits and force you to go bankrupt?" Since no one really knows what unemployment will be at the end of next year, it is perfectly okay to respond, "I don't know." But the trick is to say "I don't know" without a trace of embarrassment or bother. Next, try to answer some part of the question even if it is tangential, for example, "What I do know is that we work hard on improving our product line and our customer service every day so that we can continue

quarterly growth regardless of the macroeconomic outlook."
- Don't BS people. If you don't know the answer to a question that you should know, don't make up stuff. Tell them what you do know that is relevant, and get back to them in a timely manner with other info that you can provide.

If you follow the preceding rules, your question-and-answer session in your presentations will be consistent, positive elements in helping you create the overall impression of being a pretty good presenter.

Part Three

Tips, Tricks, and Other Sage Advice

24

TIME CRUNCH

How to Prepare if You Have Only . . .

ONE DAY

If I Have Only One Day to Prepare for a Presentation, What Should I Do?

One hour: Research and gather as much information as possible on the topic on which you'll be presenting. You will be tempted to spend many, many hours more than this on research, but that's a huge mistake. Additional research this late in the game is just an excuse for you to avoid doing the hard work of preparing, refining, and rehearsing your presentation. If you don't stop gathering facts after one hour, you will doom your presentation because you will waste the time necessary to do the remaining (vital) tasks.

30 minutes: Make a bulleted list of points—10 words or less each—of every major message point you might want to communicate to that audience.

30 minutes: Email the bullet points to any friends who might be in the audience or who have a similar mind-set to audience members. Additionally, call three people and tell them your options for messages. Ask the friends you've emailed and called for a list of their top five messages on this topic.

30 minutes: Narrow your 20 to 30 message points down to your top 5 points.

One hour: Think of a case study, an example, and a story involving a conversation you had with a real client, colleague, or customer involving this issue for each of the five points.

30 minutes: Write down every fact, number, or data point that is absolutely essential for you to present. Eliminate anything that is not 100 percent imperative.

30 minutes: Type a simple outline that has five key bullet points—one for each of your main messages. Underneath each one, include a couple of words to remind you of your stories, examples, and case studies. Finally, put at most one or two essential facts under each message point. Make sure the outline is in large font of at least 20 points *and* that the entire outline fits on a single sheet of paper.

30 minutes: Create one PowerPoint slide for each key message point. It's preferable to use a picture or image instead of text; but if you're going to use text, limit each slide to three bullet points with no more than five words for each.

One hour: Create a document that has all of your remaining factors, numbers, slides, charts, graphs, messages, and data points relating to your topic. Organize in either bullet point or paragraph fashion, whatever is easier and faster for you. This is not for you to read during the presentation; it will be something you hand out to audience members afterwards to help those who want to learn more, and to impress the rest that you did your homework.

One hour: Rehearse your presentation by going through the whole thing as if you were delivering it for real to your intended audience. Record the entire presentation using a webcam, flip camera, cell phone camera, digital camera, or other video recording device that's available to you. Watch the video and figure out what you like and don't like. Do this as many times as possible in one hour (even if it's just once).

15 minutes: Make any final adjustments to your outline, examples, facts, and slides.

45 minutes: Do final video rehearsal. Record and watch yourself. Do as many times as possible until your time is used up. Preferably, don't stop rehearsing until you like the final video of your speech.

You are now ready to deliver your presentation.

MERE HOURS

If I Have Only Two Hours to Prepare for a Presentation, What Should I Do?

20 minutes: Research and gather as much information as possible on the topic on which you will be presenting. You will be tempted to spend all of your time on research, but again, this is a huge mistake. Cut yourself off after 20 minutes—no matter what.

10 minutes: Narrow all possible message points down to your top five points.

15 minutes: Think of a case study, an example, and a story involving a conversation you had with a real client, colleague, or customer involving this issue for as many of the five points as possible.

15 minutes: Type a simple outline that has five key bullet points—one for each of your main messages—and underneath each one include a couple of words to remind you of your stories, examples, and case studies. Finally, put at most one or two essential facts under each message point. Make sure the outline is in large font of at least 20 points *and* that it all fits on a single sheet of paper.

20 minutes: Create a short document that has any of the remaining factors, numbers, slides, charts, graphs, messages, and data points related to your topic. Organize in either bullet point or paragraph fashion, whatever is easier and faster for you. This won't be anything you read during the presentation, but it will be something you hand out to audience members afterwards to help those who want to learn more—and to impress the rest with the fact that you did your homework.

20 minutes: Rehearse your presentation by going through the whole thing as if you were delivering it for real to your intended audience. Record the entire presentation (or at least the first 15 minutes' worth) with a webcam, flip camera, cell phone camera, digital camera, or any other video recording device. Watch as much as you can (at least the first five minutes' worth) of the video, and figure out what you like and don't like.

20 minutes: Make any final adjustments to your outline. Do final video rehearsal. Record and watch yourself.

Final tip: Smile and act like you have been preparing your presentation for this crowd for weeks and weeks and weeks because they are so important.

You are now ready to deliver your presentation.

MINUTES!?

If I Have Only Five Minutes to Prepare for a Presentation, What Should I Do?

Minute 1: Decide on just one important idea you want to convey to your audience.

Minute 2: Think of one good example or story you can give to make this one idea come alive.

Minute 3: Quickly grab a napkin or a scratch sheet of paper and write down a couple of words to remind you of your key point, a related example, and a few essential facts that you might not otherwise remember.

Minute 4: Silently practice giving the first part of your speech in your own head (I'm assuming you are in the same room as where your presentation will take place, that there are people in the room, and that your boss just alerted you that you will be called upon in five minutes to give a quick update on something).

Minute 5: Look at your outline one more time; think of what your first sentence will be when you start; and then listen to what's happening right now in the room in case you have to react.

Other key considerations for giving presentations with only five minutes' advance notice:

- Never mention or complain that you had only five minutes to prepare. You don't want to hear about other people's problems, and they don't want to hear about yours.
- Smile and focus on radiating confidence and comfort—even if you are scared to death and afraid you are going to make a royal a#@ out of yourself.
- Realize that if people know you were given only five minutes to make a presentation, they will grade you on a curve in your favor. Since expectations are lower, it will actually be easier to make a pretty good impression.
- Remember that it's okay to glance down at your notes, though you preferably aren't holding them in your hands.

- Don't shoot your eyes upwards looking for answers from the heavens, and don't stare down at your notes either. It is critically important that you make eye contact with your audience. Your whole presentation may only last four minutes, but Lincoln's Gettysburg Address was only three minutes. Make the most of whatever time you have to present.
- Don't put pressure on yourself to remember everything your department has done in the last fiscal year. Instead, just focus on one or two very important points.
- If someone asks you a question you don't know, don't act flustered (even if you are). Instead, inform them with a confident and authoritative smile on your face how and when you will get them this information; and then deliver it, perhaps via email by close of business today.
- Don't look relieved when your presentation is over (even though you will be). Instead, look and act as if there is no place else in the entire world you would rather be than standing in front of this crowd presenting to them. In other words, act like you are having fun, even if you think it's torture.

25

DEVELOP THE ART

What's Another Good Way to Keep My Presenting Skills from Becoming Awful?

Use them as frequently as possible. I know that you don't love to give speeches—and you aren't a preacher who's putting speaking skills to use every Sunday morning—but try not to let them rot away from underuse. After all, how good will your golf game become if you play golf only once every five years? Probably not very good. However, if you play golf once every three weeks, you'll at least know, more or less, how you will do next time you are on the links. I'm not suggesting you spend every free night giving speeches at the local toastmasters club, but you could look for some opportunity to speak out once every three or four weeks. It could simply be giving a toast in front of six friends at a birthday party, or asking a question at a school board meeting. It might even just mean that you volunteer to say the pledge of allegiance at school convocation. Every time you speak in front of more than a person or two, it helps your body and mouth condition itself to surviving the nerves and tensions associated with giving presentations.

Imagine how difficult it would be to stand up and walk across the room if you sit in a chair for a whole year without getting up once. Your legs would be wobbly and weak. The same is true for giving presentations; if you wait a year in between them, you will also be wobbly and weak. You might not be an Olympic-class runner now, but you can most likely walk across the room easily because you practice walking every day. I'm not saying you have to give a presentation every single day, but the less time in between presentations—any presentations—the better.

26

TIME TRAP

*What Are Common Time Wasters to
Avoid When Preparing for My
Presentation?*

Giving presentations is in some ways very similar to managing your personal finances and losing lots of weight; there is a lot of bad advice out there, and anyone can have an opinion.

I've tried to gather all the advice that, if followed, would waste lots of your valuable time. The following are instructions that you will *not* have to follow because they are either bad advice for all presenters or bad advice for you, in particular, to meeting your goal of giving a pretty good presentation:

- **"Memorize the first minute of your presentation."**

  This is tough to do and isn't worth the effort. It's a great way to create stage fright and panic.
- **"Practice your presentation while looking at yourself in a mirror."**

  Another waste of time that's guaranteed to make you obsess over your crooked nose or receding hairline. The one thing you don't have to do when giving a speech is look at yourself.
- **"Visualize your audience naked."**

  Terrible advice. Depending on your audience, this is either too disgusting or too distracting.
- **"Limit your PowerPoint to no more than 10 slides."**

  More than 10 slides won't necessarily help you, but in the real world, people who use this artificial constraint of 10 end up cramming four slides' worth of content onto one slide; and then nobody can read it!

- **"Write out your entire speech word for word."**

  There is no need to do this. Just have a simple one-page outline using bullet points.

- **"Obsess over the size and color of your Power-Point font."**

  Generally, a complete waste of time.

- **"Worry about moving your hands."**

  Actually, you should move your hands when you talk. Only nervous people freeze or hold their hands when they speak.

- **"Cram every single fact, number, and data point on what you and your department have done in the past six months into your presentation."**

  If the people to whom you are presenting really had to know every single thing you did, then they'd have your job. It's your job to tell them only what's truly important to them.

- **"Brainstorm on every single possible question that could be asked by an audience member."**

  Sure, you need to be able to answer most questions; but there are an infinite number of questions that could be asked. It's a waste of time to worry about hypothetical questions when the bigger danger is that you haven't prepared anything interesting or memorable to present in the first place.

- **"Worry about the sound of your voice."**

  Nobody cares or notices your voice. As long as you can be heard and understood, then it is highly unlikely that your voice is a problem with which you should concern yourself. Besides, there is nothing you can do (easily) about your voice!

- **"Obsess over special effects, dissolves, and builds in your PowerPoint."**

  Even if people notice your special effects, they won't relate it to the messages of your presentation. Special effects usually become a big black-hole time drain. Far better to spend your time preparing something interesting to say.

- **"Put off giving your presentation until you are more seasoned or experienced."**

  Quit conning yourself. Giving presentations makes a person seasoned and experienced.

- **"Continue gathering more and more research."**

  Enough already! Chances are that you already have enough research and raw facts. The longer you stay stuck in the mode of gathering data, the less time you have for processing, shaping, highlighting, and preparing stories about the data and rehearsing your presentations.

- **"Use a thesaurus to find big words."**

  This is great if you want to look like a pompous fool. Use the simplest, shortest words you can think of.

Basically, doing anything that distracts you from focusing on a handful of key points—with examples and stories to make each point come alive and delivered in a conversational manner—is a total waste of time.

27

---

10 Public Speaking Do's and Don'ts

DO the following:
1. Be interesting.
2. Be passionate.
3. Tell stories.
4. Give examples.
5. Cite case studies.
6. Look at the audience.
7. Let people ask questions anytime.
8. Tell people why they should give a da*&!
9. Move your head, hands, and body.
10. Finish on time (or early).

DON'T do the following:
1. Read your speech.
2. Do a data dump.
3. Show complex slides with lots of words and small graphics.
4. Stare at your slides and avoid your audience.
5. Be abstract.
6. Use big, complex words.
7. Use jargon.
8. Be monotone.
9. Be boring.
10. Go over your allotted time.

28

TRUST ME ON THIS

Terrible Ideas

Things you will be tempted to do because they seem like they will make your presentation easier but are actually TERRIBLE IDEAS:

1. **Have a glass of booze.** Yes, it might appear to make you more relaxed, but it will make it harder to recall information, make you appear sweaty, and people will smell your breath and form a lifelong impression of you being a drunkard.

2. **Wing it because you want to seem fresh and not over rehearsed.** Horrible idea. You are likely to go blank, stammer, and then drone on with boring information. Don't do it.

3. **Read your speech word-for-word.** Impossible for amateurs, so don't even attempt.

4. **Wait until the night before the presentation to start preparing it.** Start as far in advance as possible, preferably by just jotting down notes on ideas, stories, and examples (don't worry about writing full sentences or paragraphs).

5. **Put all your notes on a PowerPoint slide.** Instead, put your notes on a piece of paper.

6. **Practice in front of a mirror.** Again, you will only get distracted by the shape of your nose and your receding hairline.

7. **Apologize for not having prepared a better presentation.** Nobody cares about you; just give them the best you can.

8. **Eliminate stories and examples because you are short on time.** Wretched mistake. Keep the stories, and shorten the number of data points.

9. **Speak faster than usual so that you can finish in a hurry and sit down.** This only makes you look nervous, foolish, and amateurish. Speak slower than usual.

10. **Search for one friendly face in the audience to look at the whole time.** Great, now everyone else in the audience feels ignored and will feel free to ignore you.

29

"My" Final Speaking Tip

Be Interesting

I'm often asked, "TJ, any final tips for me? I have to give a presentation tomorrow, and I still don't know exactly what to say or what I am going to do."

If you want to give a pretty good presentation, the answer is simple: just make sure you have one interesting idea in it. You may be thinking, "That's ridiculous! I have dozens and dozens of ideas, facts, and numbers in my presentation." Yes, but how many of them are interesting, significant, or memorable?

The sad fact is that most people give dreadful presentations because they didn't present a single interesting idea—not one! If you don't believe me, then try to name one interesting idea you heard from any of the last five presenters you saw.

So if you want to be a little bit lazy and still give a pretty good presentation, then I advise you to put away the complex graphs and charts, forget the complicated video inserts, and toss the three-ring binder handouts. Instead, focus what little prep time you have on making sure you have one legitimately attention-grabbing and memorable idea for the audience. Then explain it by using concrete examples and possibly a story involving a conversation you had with a real colleague, client, or friend. Make sure the point you are making is interesting and relevant, and something that might motivate your audience to take some action or at least think about something differently.

If you do this, then you will give a pretty good presentation—no matter how many other fumbles you commit. Most presenters have the following attitude: "I know that nothing I have to say to you is remotely interesting, so I will just blow through all of the boring data as quickly as possible, and as long as you don't interrupt me we can all get out of here on time."

You, however, can stand out from the pack of awful presenters, by breaking this paradigm simply by presenting a single interesting idea.

30

A FINAL WORD

I respect your decision to not make it your goal to become a world-class professional speaker. It's okay, really. But I do want to leave you with a story of a young man who was quite similar to you. Many decades ago, he was in college and had to take a public speaking class. Public speaking really wasn't his thing, and he certainly didn't consider himself to be a natural-born presenter. Sure enough, he went through the course in the way you would expect. He slogged through and got a C. (I guess you could say his teacher considered him good enough to give a "pretty good presentation.")

The funny thing is that this same guy went into a career where he had to speak a lot. And then one day he went to Washington and gave his "I Have a Dream Speech" and went down in history as having given the greatest and most influential speech of the 20th century. So if you think of yourself as only capable of giving a pretty good presentation, then you are in good company; Martin Luther King, Jr., was also in the same boat. There's nothing wrong with giving a pretty good presentation, but you already have all of the innate skills you need to be a great speaker.

Good luck with all of your future presentations!

About the Author

TJ Walker is the founder of TJ Walker Speaking (www .tjwalker.com), an online presentation training company. Walker is the author of the *USA Today* number one best seller, *TJ Walker's Secret to Foolproof Presentations*. In 2009, Walker set the Guinness Book of World Records for speaking on the most talk radio shows in a 24-hour period (96 programs). As CEO of Media Training Worldwide (www.mediatrainingworldwide.com), Walker has trained tens of thousands of clients including Presidents of countries, US Senators, CEOs, Prime Ministers, Members of Parliament, Super Bowl winners, Nobel Peace Prize winners, and Miss Universe winners. Walker is a frequent news commentator on speaking and media issues and has been on all major US cable and broadcast TV networks. His daily Internet TV show on speaking issues can be seen at www.TJWalker.com/blog.

PRESENTATION NOTES